STEP-BY-STEP

Puddings & Desserts

STEP-BY-STEP

Puddings & Desserts

CARA HOBDAY

This edition printed in 1995 for:
Shooting Star Press Inc
230 Fifth Avenue – Suite 1212
New York, NY 10001

Shooting Star Press books are available at special discounts for bulk purchases for sales promotions, premiums, fund-raising, or educational use. Special edition or book excerpts can also be created to specification. For details contact: Special Sales Director, Shooting Star Press Inc., 230 Fifth Avenue, Suite 1212, New York, NY 10001

ISBN 1-57335-007-9

Produced by Haldane Mason, London

Printed in Italy

Acknowledgements:
Art Direction: Ron Samuels
Editor: Joanna Swinnerton
Series Design: Pedro & Frances Prá-Lopez/Kingfisher Design
Page Design: Somewhere Creative
Photography: Iain Bagwell
Styling: Rachel Jukes
Home Economist: Cara Hobday

Photographs on pages 6, 20, 34, 48 & 62 reproduced by permission of
ZEFA Picture Library (UK) Ltd.

Note:
Unless otherwise stated, milk is assumed to be full-fat, eggs are AA large, and pepper is freshly ground black pepper.

Contents

CHAPTER ONE

Quick & Easy

You may find yourself in a situation where a dessert needs to be rustled up in a hurry – for unexpected guests, family meals, or hungry teenagers – and that is when you turn to this section! Here are six versions of wonderful desserts that are ready in no time.

A well-chosen supply of staples makes it easier to put last-minute creations together – stock up on brandysnaps, ratafia cookies or macaroons, pound cake, ladyfingers, eggs, longlife cream, canned fruit, raisins, dried fruit, light corn syrup and canned custard.

A quick dessert can be made by baking fruit – try apples, pears or figs, drizzled with a little honey – or simply combine fruit with cream and custard for a quick fruit fool. Some canned fruits make excellent alternatives to fresh, especially if you are cooking or baking. I never hesitate to use canned blackcurrants, apricots, raspberries or mangoes.

Opposite: With a little imagination a delicious pudding can often be made in very little time from the most basic ingredients.

STEP 1

STEP 2

STEP 3

STEP 5

CHERRY CLAFOUTIS

This is a hot dessert that is simple and quick to put together. Try the batter with other seasonal or canned fruits. Apricots and plums are especially delicious.

SERVES 6

1 cup all-purpose flour
4 eggs, lightly beaten
2 tbsp superfine sugar
pinch of salt
2¹/₂ cups milk
butter for greasing
1 pound black cherries, fresh or canned,
    pitted
3 tbsp brandy
1 tbsp sugar to decorate

1 Sift the flour into a large bowl. Make a well in the center and add the eggs, sugar and salt.

2 Draw in the flour, and whisk.

3 Add the milk, and whisk until smooth.

4 Butter a 3¹/₂-cup ovenproof serving dish, and pour in half of the batter.

5 Spoon the cherries over the batter and pour the remaining batter over the top. Sprinkle the brandy over the batter.

6 Bake in a preheated oven at 350°F for 40 minutes.

7 Remove from the oven. Just before serving, sprinkle over the sugar. Serve warm, from the dish.

SERVING SUGGESTION

As this dessert is served straight from the oven, it is worth using a decorative dish. There are several types of attractive ovenproof serving dishes available to buy, including plain colored ceramic and enamel dishes. Some china dishes, but not all, are ovenproof, so be sure to check this when you buy. I would recommend stoneware, a type of heavy porcelain, which is ovenproof and usually decorated very attractively.

STEP 1

STEP 2

STEP 3

STEP 7

SCOTCH MIST

In our family, crannachan, as it is more commonly known, has always been called Scotch Mist, and now I know the origin of it – good Scotch whisky! This is a wholesome dish, which improves if left overnight.

SERVES 4–6

generous 3 cups raspberries, fresh or frozen
3 tbsp Scotch whisky
1¼ cups heavy cream
4 tbsp heather honey (if not available, use
   clear honey)
⅓ cup oatmeal

1 Reserve scant 1 cup of the raspberries, and put the rest into a bowl with the Scotch whisky. Set aside.

2 Whip the cream until softly stiff.

3 Stir in the honey and oatmeal. If the cream turns soft, whip again until stiff.

4 Spoon a few raspberries into the bottom of each serving glass, or spoon half the raspberries into the bottom of a large glass bowl.

5 Spoon half the cream mixture over the raspberries, then add the remaining raspberries.

6 Spoon the remaining cream over the top. Chill for at least 1 hour, preferably overnight.

7 Mash the reserved raspberries with a wooden spoon, or blend them in a blender, then press them through a strainer.

8 When ready to serve, pour a little of the strained raspberries over each glass, or over the whole bowl.

OATMEAL

Although there are different types of oatmeal available, they are all made from the same thing; the only difference is how much the oats have been milled. I always use the medium-cut one that still has some fine, floury content, as opposed to the slightly more gritty version with no "dust."

STEP 1

STEP 4

STEP 5

STEP 6

CREPES SUZETTE

*They don't come much more French than this one! This classic dessert is
served in restaurants everywhere.*

SERVES 4–6

1 cup all-purpose flour
1 egg
1 egg yolk
1¼ cups milk
¼ cup melted butter
grated rind of 1 orange
1 cup granulated sugar
²/₃ cup water
pared rind of 1 orange
melted butter, for frying
juice of 1 orange
1 cup orange-flavored liqueur
1 orange, peeled and segmented

1 Sift the flour into a bowl, and make a well in the center. Add the egg, egg yolk, milk and butter, and draw in the flour. Whisk to a smooth batter. Stir in the orange rind.

2 Leave the pancake batter to rest for 30 minutes.

3 Put the sugar and water into a saucepan, and bring to a slow boil. Add the orange rind, and cook slowly until the syrup coats the back of a spoon, about 5 minutes. Set aside.

4 Meanwhile, brush a skillet or pancake pan with a little melted butter, and place over a medium heat. Tilt the skillet to one side, and pour in about ¼ cup of the batter. Tilt the pan in the opposite direction immediately, so that the whole base is covered in batter.

5 After about 1 minute, or when the pancake is dry on top, toss it and cook the other side for another minute. Make 8–12 pancakes, and keep warm in a low oven. Place 2 pancakes on each warmed serving plate, either flat or folded.

6 Reheat the syrup, and stir in the orange juice, ²/₃ cup of the liqueur and the segmented orange. Pour a little over each serving plate.

7 Heat the remaining liqueur slowly in a small pouring pan. It may ignite itself, but if it does not, set a lighted match to it, and pour over the pancakes immediately. This is most effective if done at the serving table. You can warm the liqueur in the kitchen, then take it to the table and ignite it. Blow out the flames immediately.

CHOCOLATE COCONUT LAYER

This is a rich, easy dessert for chocolate-lovers. If you can't wait, it can be eaten immediately, still warm and gooey, or it can be chilled until set and served with coffee.

STEP 1

SERVES 6–8

7 squares dark chocolate, broken into pieces
1¼ cups cream cheese
²/₃ cup grated or shredded coconut
2 cups graham crackers, crumbled

TO DECORATE:
confectioners' sugar
coconut curls or shredded coconut

1 Melt the chocolate in a heatproof bowl set over a saucepan of barely simmering water for about 10 minutes. Do not let the water splash into the bowl, as it will affect the texture of the chocolate.

2 Turn off the heat. Add the cream cheese to the chocolate, and stir till well blended and smooth.

3 Remove the bowl from the saucepan, and stir in the grated or shredded coconut.

4 Place half of the cracker crumbs on the bottom of a shallow 4½-cup dish.

5 Layer with half the chocolate mixture, then another layer of the remaining cracker crumbs, finishing with a layer of the remaining chocolate mixture. Chill for 2 hours.

6 Dust with confectioners' sugar and coconut curls or shredded coconut before serving.

COCONUT CURLS

If using a fresh coconut, drain the milk, and split the coconut apart using a hammer. Remove the flesh from the shell in large pieces. To make the curls, peel down one side of each piece of coconut flesh with a peeler, and use the resulting curls for decoration.

TIPS

This can be kept for up to 5 days in the refrigerator, but remember to cover the dish carefully so that the dessert doesn't absorb other flavors.

If you prefer, you can make individual desserts using 6–8 ramekins or glasses instead of one large bowl. Distribute the ingredients evenly among the ramekins.

STEP 2

STEP 3

STEP 4

STEP 4

STEP 5

STEP 7

STEP 8

RUM & RAISIN CRUNCH

I based this recipe on old-fashioned brandysnaps and cream, which I can remember eating at country fairs as a child. You can use ready-made brandysnaps, or make your own with this recipe.

SERVES 4

BRANDYSNAPS:
$^1/_2$ *cup butter*
$^1/_2$ *cup superfine sugar*
$^1/_3$ *cup light corn syrup*
$^3/_4$ *cup sifted all-purpose flour*
$^1/_2$ *tsp ground ginger*

RUM & RAISIN CREAM:
$^2/_3$ *cup raisins*
5 tbsp dark rum
5 tbsp water
$^2/_3$ *cup whipping cream*
$^1/_4$ *cup Ricotta or full-fat soft cheese*
$^1/_4$ *cup sifted confectioners' sugar*
$^1/_4$ *cup ground almonds*
$^1/_4$ *tsp almond extract*
2 egg whites
6 brandysnaps, lightly crushed

1 To make the brandysnaps, put the butter, sugar and syrup into a saucepan, and heat slowly until melted.

2 Remove from the heat, and mix in the flour and ginger until blended. Drop teaspoonfuls of the mixture onto a cookie sheet, leaving space to spread. Bake in a preheated oven at 350°F for about 8 minutes until golden-brown.

3 Chill 4 ramekins or a serving bowl.

4 Put the raisins, rum and water into a saucepan, and bring to a boil. Simmer for 5 minutes, then leave to rest for 20 minutes.

5 Whip the cream.

6 Press the soft cheese through a strainer and stir in the confectioners' sugar.

7 Fold in the whipped cream, ground almonds and extract. Beat the egg whites, and fold them into the mixture.

8 Drain the raisins, and stir them into the mixture with the crushed brandysnaps.

9 Spoon into the chilled dishes. Chill for at least 30 minutes.

STEP 1: Belle Hélène

STEP 2: Belle Hélène

STEP 1: Framboises

STEP 2: Framboises

COUPE AU CHOCOLAT

On a hot summer's day there is nothing nicer than sitting at a pavement café and choosing from a whole menu of ice cream coupes, all of which are beautifully presented and delicious. Here are some quick ideas to liven up chocolate ice cream.

EACH RECIPE SERVES 4

COUPE BELLE HELENE:
1 cup granulated sugar
1 cup water
3 pears, peeled, quartered and cored
4 squares dark chocolate
chocolate ice cream
whipped heavy cream (optional)

1 Put the sugar and water into a saucepan, and bring to a boil. Simmer for 5 minutes, and add the pears. Simmer gently for 10 minutes, or until the pears are tender. Very ripe pears will not take as long. Set the pears aside, and drain off half of the syrup.

2 Break up the chocolate, and add it to the syrup in the saucepan. Stir until smooth, about 3–4 minutes.

3 To serve, put 3 scoops of ice cream into each serving dish or coupe, and spoon over 3 pear quarters. Pour a little chocolate syrup over the whole, and pipe some cream on top, if liked.

COUPE AUX FRAMBOISES:
8-ounce can raspberries in syrup
  or 1¹/₃ cups raspberries, fresh or frozen
about 3 tbsp confectioners' sugar

chocolate ice cream
whipped heavy cream (optional)
ice cream wafers

1 If you are using canned raspberries, purée them in a blender or food processor, or mash them well with a wooden spoon.

2 If using fresh raspberries, purée them in a blender or food processor, or mash them well with a wooden spoon, and press through a strainer. Sift in confectioners' sugar to taste.

3 To serve, put 3 scoops of ice cream in each chilled serving dish or coupe, and pour the raspberry sauce over the top. Pipe whipped cream on the top if liked, and serve with wafers.

VARIATION

Other instant sauces can be whipped up by puréeing a can of blackcurrants in syrup or strawberries in syrup, and serving with ice cream of your choice.

CHAPTER TWO

Hot Puddings

A cold winter's night is the best time to enjoy a hot pudding without feeling guilty – after all, we have to keep the cold out somehow! There is no better way to do this than with a comforting Italian Bread & Butter Pudding, and Granny Bob's Chocolate Pudding is guaranteed to warm a few hearts. Even if you don't need to count the calories, you may be pleased to know that the Raisin & Nut Pudding has very little cholesterol.

Not all hot puddings need be substantial and filling: if you prefer a lighter hot pudding, try the Magic Lemon Pudding or Almond Pancakes with Fruit Coulis.

Opposite: *Hot puddings are the ultimate comfort food, and chocolate is often a key ingredient. Use a high-quality chocolate for the best results.*

STEP 1

STEP 2

STEP 3

STEP 4

MAGIC LEMON PUDDING

This light dessert magically separates in the oven to form a thick lemon sauce base and a spongy topping. My mother was baking this in the 1950s, and now it has become fashionable again!

SERVES 4–6

⅓ cup granulated sugar
¼ cup all-purpose flour
2 egg yolks
1 tbsp butter
finely grated rind of 1 lemon
4 tbsp lemon juice
1 cup milk
2 egg whites

TO DECORATE:
confectioners' sugar
grated lemon rind

1 Sift the sugar and flour together into a bowl.

2 Stir in the egg yolks, butter, and lemon rind and juice. Beat together thoroughly.

3 Stir in the milk, and whisk well.

4 Beat the egg whites until stiff and fold in well.

5 Spoon the mixture into a 4-cup ovenproof serving dish.

6 Put the dish into a roasting pan half-filled with water, and bake in a preheated oven at 350°F for 35 minutes.

7 Sprinkle with grated lemon rind, and dust with confectioners' sugar. Serve immediately from the dish.

BEATING EGG WHITES

When beating egg whites, start slowly, using a figure-of-eight motion, until the whites are a mass of bubbles, then speed up gradually. If using a balloon whisk, you may find it comfortable to rest the bowl on your left hip and beat with the right arm, or vice versa. Electric whisks are a lot quicker, but they do not achieve such a large volume from the egg whites as a traditional hand whisk would. Using a copper bowl reacts with the egg whites to make them stronger, more long-lasting and resilient, which is useful when the egg whites are being folded into a mixture. Make sure the bowl is completely dry and free of grease, as even a little water or grease will make the whites harder to beat to a good "froth."

STEP 2

STEP 3

STEP 4

STEP 5

GRANNY BOB'S
CHOCOLATE PUDDING

A deliciously moist pudding, served piping hot to the table. Softly whipped cream is a wonderful addition.

SERVES 4–6

1/4 cup softened butter
1/2 cup superfine sugar
2 squares dark chocolate, broken into pieces
2 eggs, lightly beaten
1 cup self-rising flour

SAUCE:
1 1/4 cups milk
1/4 cup butter
2 squares dark chocolate, broken into pieces
3 tbsp granulated sugar
2 tbsp light corn syrup

1 Grease a 4 1/2-cup pudding mold. In a separate bowl, beat the butter and sugar together until pale.

2 Meanwhile, melt the chocolate in a bowl set over a pan of barely simmering water. This should take about 10 minutes. Stir into the butter mixture.

3 Beat in the eggs, one at a time, beating well after each addition.

4 Sift the flour into the bowl, and fold in thoroughly.

5 Put all the sauce ingredients into a saucepan, and heat through slowly, without boiling, for about 10 minutes, until the chocolate has melted. Whisk well to combine.

6 Pour the sponge mixture into the greased pudding mold, and pour the sauce over the top.

7 Bake in a preheated oven at 375°F for about 40 minutes, and serve piping hot from the bowl, or turned out on to a serving plate.

MELTING CHOCOLATE

Chocolate must be melted slowly in order to prevent it from "seizing", which results in the chocolate being very granular and unworkable. To avoid this, chocolate must not come into contact with droplets of water, or be heated to too high a temperature too quickly – treat chocolate with care.

STEP 2

STEP 4

STEP 5

STEP 6

ITALIAN BREAD & BUTTER PUDDING

This was created at one of those times when I was forced to improvise through lack of ingredients! Isn't it strange how those desserts are often the best?

SERVES 4–6

¹/₃ cup softened unsalted butter
7 slices white bread
¹/₂ cup raisins
2 tbsp almond liqueur, such as Amaretto
1 cup coarsely crushed ratafias, macaroons,
   or amaretti cookies
3 tbsp cut candied peel
2¹/₂ cups milk
¹/₄ tsp vanilla extract
¹/₃ cup superfine sugar
2 eggs, lightly beaten
¹/₃ cup soft light brown sugar

1 Grease a 10 × 8 in.-baking dish with some of the butter.

2 Spread the remaining butter onto the bread.

3 Combine the raisins, liqueur and 2 tablespoons of water in a small saucepan, and bring to a gentle boil, then set aside for 30 minutes.

4 Leave the crusts on the bread slices, and cut each slice diagonally into 4 pieces. Use half of the bread to make a layer in the bottom of the dish, overlapping in rows.

5 Sprinkle with half of the ratafias, half the soaked raisins and half the candied peel. Repeat with the remaining half of the ingredients.

6 Heat the milk through slowly with the vanilla extract, until the surface quivers, and it is nearly boiling. Remove from the heat, and stir in the superfine sugar and eggs. Spoon the milk mixture over the whole bread dish. Sprinkle over the brown sugar.

7 Bake in a preheated oven at 350°F for 30 minutes. Serve immediately, piping hot from the dish.

VARIATIONS

For a variation, try adding dried fruit, such as apricots, cherries or dates, to the Bread & Butter Pudding. Another delicious alternative is to use malted milk, made up from malted hot-drink powder, in place of the ordinary milk.

RAISIN & NUT PUDDING

This a deliciously moist, low-fat pudding. The sauce is in the center of the pudding, and will spill out when the pudding is cut. Serve with custard for a richer pudding.

STEP 3

SERVES 6–8

¾ *cup raisins*
generous ½ *cup corn oil, plus a little for brushing*
generous ½ *cup superfine sugar*
¼ *cup ground almonds*
2 eggs, lightly beaten
1½ *cups self-rising flour*

SAUCE:
½ *cup chopped walnuts*
½ *cup ground almonds*
1¼ *cups milk (semi-skimmed may be used)*
4 tbsp granulated sugar

1 Put the raisins in a saucepan with ½ cup water. Bring to a boil, then remove from the heat. Leave to steep for 10 minutes, then drain.

2 Whisk together the oil, sugar and ground almonds until thick and syrupy; this will need about 8 minutes of beating (on medium speed if using an electric whisk).

3 Add the eggs, one at a time, beating well after each addition.

4 Combine the flour and raisins. Stir into the mixture.

5 Brush a 4-cup pudding mold with oil, or line with baking parchment.

6 Put all the sauce ingredients into a saucepan. Bring to a boil, stir and simmer for 10 minutes.

7 Transfer the sponge mixture to the greased mold, and pour on the hot sauce. Place on a metal cookie sheet.

8 Bake in a preheated oven at 340°F for about 1 hour. Lay a piece of baking parchment across the top if it starts to brown too fast.

9 Let cool for 2–3 minutes in the mold before turning out onto a serving plate.

STEP 4

STEP 5

RAISINS

I always soak raisins before baking them, as they retain their moisture nicely and you taste the flavor of them instead of biting on a dried-out raisin.

STEP 6

STEP 2

STEP 4

STEP 5

STEP 6

ALMOND PANCAKES WITH FRUIT COULIS

I designed this dessert for the times when something hot, but not necessarily heavy or too filling, is needed.

SERVES 4–8

1/4 cup slivered almonds
1 cup all-purpose flour
1 egg
1 egg yolk
1 1/4 cups milk
2 tbsp melted butter
4 tbsp ground almonds, lightly toasted
1/4 tsp almond extract
oil for brushing
1 1/2 cups frozen mixed summer fruits, such as redcurrants, blackcurrants and raspberries
2 tbsp confectioners' sugar
14-ounce can guavas in syrup, or other fruit of your choice

1 Spread out the slivered almonds on a baking sheet, and toast them in a preheated oven at 350°F for 3 minutes.

2 Sift the flour into a bowl, and make a well in the center. Add the egg, egg yolk, milk, melted butter, ground almonds and almond extract. Whisk well to combine. Let rest for 30 minutes.

3 Brush a skillet or pancake pan with oil, and place over a medium heat. Tilt the skillet in one direction, and pour in 1/4 cup of the batter. Tilt in the opposite direction immediately, so that the batter covers the whole bottom of the skillet. After 1–2 minutes, or when the top of the pancake starts to dry out, toss it, and cook on the other side for about 1 minute. Repeat with the remaining batter.

4 Transfer the pancakes to a cookie sheet lined with baking parchment. Cover and keep warm in a preheated oven at 300°F.

5 Blend the mixed fruit in a blender or food processor, or mash it well by hand, with 2 tablespoons of water. Press through a strainer, and stir in the confectioners' sugar. Warm the fruit coulis through over a medium heat.

6 Warm the guavas through, in their own syrup, over a medium heat without boiling.

7 Fold each pancake twice, and place 1 or 2 on each serving plate. Lift the top layer of each pancake and spoon in the warmed guavas. Decorate with the toasted almonds and pour a little fruit coulis onto each dessert plate.

STEP 2

STEP 3

STEP 4

STEP 6

TARTE TATIN

The classic Tarte Tatin, or upside-down cake, is made with apples; here I have used pears which, I'm sure you will agree, are equally delicious!

SERVES 4–6

DOUGH:
½ cup softened unsalted butter
⅓ cup superfine sugar
1 egg, lightly beaten
2 cups all-purpose flour
salt

PEAR TOPPING:
2 tbsp butter
⅓ cup light brown sugar
1 tbsp lemon juice
2 pounds eating pears

1 First make the dough. Beat the butter and superfine sugar together until light and fluffy.

2 Add the egg, and beat well. Add the flour gradually with a pinch of salt, and mix to a smooth dough. Knead lightly for 5 minutes. Wrap and chill for at least 2 hours.

3 Meanwhile, line the bottom of a 9-in. cake pan with baking parchment, and spread half the butter and brown sugar over the bottom.

4 Add the lemon juice to a large bowl of water. Peel, core and quarter the pears, putting them into the acidulated water as you go. When all the pears are prepared, drain off the water thoroughly, and pat the fruit dry with paper towels. Pack them tightly into the bottom of the cake pan.

5 Sprinkle over the remaining brown sugar and butter. Bake in a preheated oven at 425°F for 20 minutes, or until a light caramel forms.

6 Just before ready to cook, remove the dough from the refrigerator, and roll out into a 10-in. round on a floured counter. Work quickly at this stage, so that the butter in the dough does not melt. Use plenty of flour on both the counter and the rolling pin. Do not worry about making the round very neat as the tarte is inverted, so any wrinkles will not show. Place the dough over the pears.

7 Bake in a preheated oven at 400°F for about 20 minutes, or until well browned.

8 Remove from the oven, and invert on a warmed serving plate. Serve at once with clotted cream or ice cream.

CHAPTER THREE

Cold Puddings

Sometimes a substantial cold dessert is required for a party or buffet or to round off a light meal. Here are a few ideas, all of which can be made ahead and stored in the refrigerator for up to 3 days. The Summer Pudding will last longer, up to 6 days.

Personally, I love a good Sherry Trifle, and there are few people who don't, but everybody has their own recipe and this is mine. Trifles often have fruit gelatin set in the bottom, which is a variation on the original recipe; I'm not very keen on this, so my recipe follows the traditional path, which I think you will prefer.

Summer Pudding will become a perennial favorite. It is best made in late summer when fresh blackberries are available – and, in some areas, wild strawberries – which add lots of flavor. Serve simply with clotted or light cream.

Tiramisù has many imitators, but the only way to get the unique flavor and texture is to use Mascarpone cheese, stirred into the cream; otherwise it becomes simply a chocolate trifle.

Opposite: *The simplest ingredients can make the most elegant puddings. Choose ingredients that are at their peak for the best flavor and appearance.*

STEP 1

STEP 2

STEP 3

STEP 5

SUMMER PUDDING

Use whatever summer fruit you have available. Strawberries do not give such a good result, but cherries are delicious when included in the mixture. Good quality frozen fruit can now be bought all year round.

SERVES 4–6

2 pounds mixed summer fruit, such as
blackberries, redcurrants, blackcurrants,
raspberries, loganberries and cherries
³/₄ cup superfine sugar
8 small slices white bread
clotted cream or light cream, to serve

1 Stir the fruit and sugar together in a large saucepan, cover and bring to a boil. Simmer for 10 minutes, stirring once.

2 Cut the crusts off the bread slices.

3 Line a 4¹/₂-cup pudding mold with the bread slices.

4 Add the fruit and as much of the cooking juices as will fit into the bread-lined mold.

5 Cover the fruit with the remaining bread slices.

6 Put the pudding mold onto a large plate or a shallow cookie sheet. Place a plate on top, and weigh it down with cans.

7 Chill overnight, or for up to 6 days.

8 When ready to serve, turn the pudding out onto a serving plate or shallow bowl, and serve cold with clotted cream or light cream.

V A R I A T I O N

To give the pudding a more lasting set, dissolve 2 envelopes or 2 tablespoons of powdered gelatin in water, and stir into the fruit mixture. This enables you to invert it on the serving plate a couple of hours before serving.

STEP 2

STEP 4

STEP 5

STEP 6

WHITE & DARK CHOCOLATE MOUSSE

Although this looks stunning, it is in fact very simple to make, with the aid of a couple of large bowls and a good hand whisk. If you like, make both white and dark chcolate curls to decorate.

SERVES 6–8

3^1/$_2$ squares dark chocolate
3^1/$_2$ squares good quality white chocolate
4 egg yolks
2 tbsp brandy
1 envelope or 1 tbsp powdered gelatin
^{1}/$_4$ cup hot water
1^1/$_4$ cups heavy cream
4 egg whites

TO DECORATE:
3^1/$_2$ squares good quality white or dark
   chocolate
1 tbsp shortening
cocoa powder

1 Break the dark and white chocolate into pieces, and put them into separate heatproof bowls. Set the bowls over saucepans of barely simmering water, and melt the chocolate.

2 When melted, remove the bowls, and beat 2 egg yolks into each, until smooth. Stir the brandy into the dark chocolate mixture. Set aside to cool, stirring the chocolate frequently.

3 Combine the gelatin and hot water in a heatproof bowl. Set over a pan of barely simmering water, and wait for it to clear, about 10 minutes. Stir half of the gelatin into each chocolate mixture until smooth.

4 Whip the cream until softly stiff, and beat the egg whites until stiff.

5 Stir half of the cream into each chocolate mixture, then fold half of the egg whites into each chocolate mixture.

6 Pour or spoon both mousses at the same time into a 3^1/$_2$-cup soufflé dish, one in each half of the dish, so that they meet in the middle, but do not run into each other. Chill until ready to serve.

7 Break the chocolate for decorating into pieces, and put into a heatproof bowl. Set over a pan of barely simmering water until melted, then stir in the shortening and pour into a small loaf pan. Chill until set, then turn out.

8 To decorate, shave large curls of chocolate from the block with a vegetable peeler. Arrange attractively on the mousse, and dust with cocoa powder.

STEP 2

STEP 3

STEP 4

STEP 5

SHERRY TRIFLE

This is a classic trifle recipe, which never fails to please. Use whatever fruit you have available, and likewise the pound cake can be replaced with ladyfingers or sponge cake.

SERVES 4–6

$^1\!/_2$ cup cornstarch
$4^1\!/_2$ cups milk
10 egg yolks
$^1\!/_2$ tsp almond extract
$^1\!/_2$ cup superfine sugar
6in. pound cake or sponge cake, sliced
2 tbsp raspberry jam
1 cup sherry, sweet or dry, depending on
   taste
$1^1\!/_2$ tbsp chopped mixed nuts
2×14-ounce cans pineapple rings
10 candied cherries

TO DECORATE:
$1^1\!/_4$ cups whipping cream
chopped angelica
slivered almonds, toasted

1 First make the custard. Blend the cornstarch in a saucepan with a little of the milk to make a paste. Add the remaining milk, and place over a medium heat. When it reaches boiling point, remove from the heat.

2 Meanwhile, beat together the egg yolks, almond extract and superfine sugar until pale. Pour on the hot milk while beating continuously. Transfer to a clean pan, and stir over a low heat for 5 minutes, or until thickened.

3 Put the slices of cake in the bottom of a glass serving bowl. Spread thinly with the raspberry jam.

4 Sprinkle the sherry and then the nuts over the cake.

5 Arrange the pineapple rings around the edge of the bowl, flat against the glass. Put 1 candied cherry in the center of each pineapple ring.

6 Pour in the cooled custard without disturbing the pineapple rings, and chill until the custard is set.

7 To decorate, whip the cream until it is of piping consistency, and pipe rosettes around the top of the trifle. Cut the angelica into squares, and top each rosette with a square. Sprinkle the toasted slivered almonds over the top, and serve.

CREME AUX MARRONS

The classic chestnut dessert is Mont Blanc, which is simply chestnuts and cream. This uses the same flavors with a bit of added zip!

STEP 1

SERVES 6

¹/₃ cup golden raisins
3 tbsp orange-flavored liqueur
finely grated rind of 1 orange
scant ¹/₄ cup granulated sugar
¹/₃ cup orange juice
1¹/₂ cups peeled chestnuts (canned or
  vacuum-packed)
1¹/₄ cups heavy cream
¹/₄ cup confectioners' sugar

TO DECORATE:
candied oranges

1 Put the golden raisins into a small saucepan with the liqueur and the orange rind. Cover and bring to a slow boil. Remove from the heat immediately, and let steep for 10 minutes.

2 Put the granulated sugar and orange juice into a clean saucepan, and bring to a boil, stirring until the sugar has dissolved. Add the chestnuts, and poach over a low to medium heat for 10 minutes. Drain the chestnuts, and reserve the cooking liquid.

3 Put the chestnuts into a blender with 3 tbsp of the cooking liquid. Blend until smooth; add more liquid if

necessary. Alternatively, mash the chestnuts, and press them through a strainer with 3 tablespoons of the cooking liquid. Add more liquid if necessary.

4 Whip the cream, and sift in the confectioners' sugar.

5 Reserving a little cream for decoration, put the cream into 1 pastry bag and the chestnut mixture into another. Pipe alternate layers of whipped cream and chestnut into 6 glasses. Alternatively, spoon into the glasses. The dessert is very rich, so small servings are fine. If you prefer, spoon in the chestnut mixture first, and top with the cream.

6 Spoon over the raisins. Decorate with chopped candied orange and a rosette of the whipped cream.

STEP 2

STEP 3

STEP 4

STEP 2

STEP 4

STEP 6

STEP 8

BANOFFI PIE

This is something that my grandmother used to make – it was delicious then, and still is now. It is becoming increasingly popular, and turns up on restaurant menus quite regularly. Thanks to the condensed milk, it is deliciously sticky.

SERVES 6–8

13-ounce can condensed milk
2 cups all-purpose flour
½ cup unsalted butter
8 tsp cold water
3 bananas
1¼ cups heavy cream
1 tsp instant coffee powder
1 tsp hot water

1 Leave the can of milk unopened, and place it in a saucepan of water, so that it is submerged. Bring the water to a boil, and boil the can for 4 hours.

2 Sift the flour into a bowl, and rub in the butter until the mixture resembles bread crumbs. Mix in the water, and bring the dough together lightly with your fingertips. Wrap in plastic wrap or baking parchment and chill for at least 30 minutes.

3 Line a 10-in. flan pan with baking parchment.

4 Roll out the dough into a 10-in. round and line the flan pan with it.

5 Bake in a preheated oven at 375°F for 15 minutes. Let cool in the pan.

6 Open the boiled can of condensed milk – if it is still hot, open it under a dishcloth. The milk will have turned to a toffee-like consistency. Spread a single layer of the "toffee" over the cooked pie shell.

7 Slice the bananas, and spread out over the toffee layer.

8 Whip the cream until softly stiff. Dissolve the instant coffee powder in the hot water, and fold into the cream.

9 Spoon or pipe the cream over the bananas. Chill until ready to serve.

BAKING DISH

If you are using a ceramic or non-metal pie dish, the pastry may not cook properly. To avoid this, preheat a metal baking sheet in the oven for 10 minutes, and place the pie shell on this in the oven.

STEP 1

STEP 2

STEP 3

STEP 4

TIRAMISU

Literally translated, this means "pick-me-up" – a kick start of coffee, chocolate and alcohol!

SERVES 6–8

24 ladyfingers or savoiardi
5 tbsp instant coffee powder
1 1/4 cups hot water
3 tbsp rum
1 1/4 cups heavy cream
1 cup Mascarpone cheese
1/3 cup confectioners' sugar
2 tbsp cocoa powder

1 Cover the bottom of a pretty serving dish with half the ladyfingers or savoiardi.

2 Combine the instant coffee powder and hot water, and soak the ladyfingers in half of the coffee and half of the rum for a few minutes.

3 Whip the cream. Stir in the Mascarpone cheese, and sift in the confectioners' sugar.

4 Spoon half the Mascarpone cheese mixture in a layer over the ladyfingers.

5 Sift half of the cocoa powder over the Mascarpone cheese mixture. Make another layer of ladyfingers in the same way, using the remaining coffee and rum, Mascarpone cheese mixture and cocoa powder.

6 Chill for at least 4 hours before serving.

HANDY HINT

Liquid instant coffee is ideal to use in place of instant coffee powder when baking. It can also be added to cakes to provide an instant coffee flavor.

CHAPTER FOUR

Light Desserts

Why is it that so many things that taste delicious are no good for your health? This needn't be so, and to prove it, I have put together some delicious, indulgent recipes that are kind to your health too. Rather than remove the good parts altogether, I have used supplements and substitutes wherever possible. Low-fat alternatives and cream substitutes are easily available from supermarkets; these include crème fraîche, fromage frais, creamy yogurts and other dairy alternatives, along with all the low-fat versions of these products. Do examine the packaging, though, as some of these products can have a similar fat and calorie content to the real thing, and need to be used in moderation.

Opposite: *Fresh fruit is often a key ingredient in light desserts. Using a combination of familiar and exotic fruits can make a dish as interesting to look at as it is to eat. Experiment with a range of ingredients to find your favorite combination.*

STEP 1

STEP 2

STEP 5

STEP 6

COEURS A LA CREME

This light dairy dessert is very well complemented by summer fruits and berries. It takes its name from the heart-shaped molds in which it is traditionally served, but can be made in anything with a few holes in it, such as a strainer lined with cheesecloth.

SERVES 4–6

1 cup 20 percent-fat (extra light) soft cheese
1¼ cups heavy cream
few drops vanilla extract
¼ cup confectioners' sugar
2 egg whites
14-ounce can apricots in syrup

1 Line 4 molds (or whatever you are using) with damp cheesecloth.

2 Press the soft cheese through a strainer.

3 Whip the cream until softly stiff, and add the vanilla extract and sugar.

4 Blend well, and stir into the soft cheese.

5 Beat the egg whites until stiff. Spoon a quarter of them into the cream, and blend well. Fold in the remaining whites.

6 Divide the mixture between the molds, and put them on a tray or plate. Let drain overnight in the refrigerator. At this stage they can be stored for up to 2 days in the refrigerator.

7 To serve, blend or process the apricots and their syrup. Alternatively, press them through a strainer. Invert the molds on a serving plate, and serve with a fruit coulis.

VARIATION

Raspberry coulis is delicious with this dessert. Blend or process a 14-ounce can of raspberries in syrup and strain. If fresh raspberries are available, put 1½ cups into a saucepan with 2 tablespoons confectioners' sugar. Simmer to dissolve the sugar, and strain. When cooled, serve with the Coeurs à la Crème.

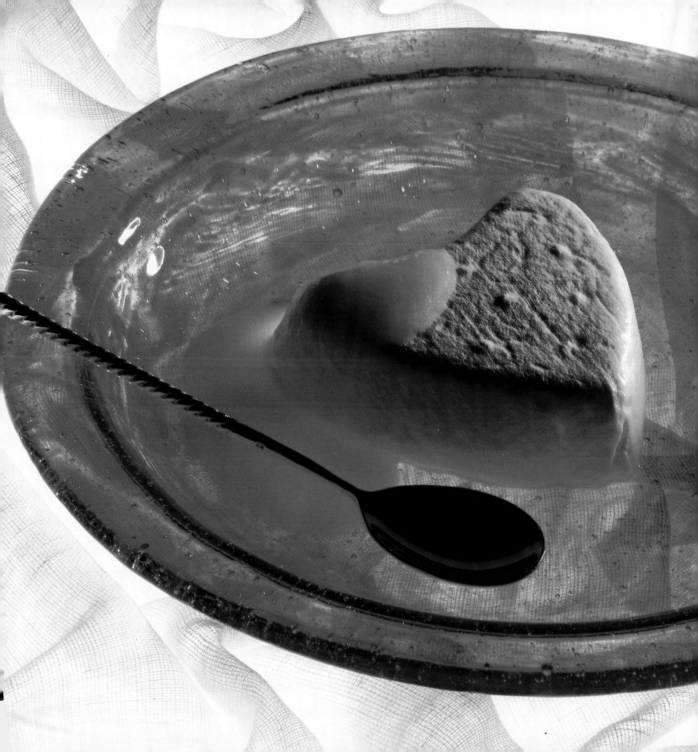

STEP 1

STEP 3

STEP 4

STEP 6

LIME FILO ROLLS

Everything can be prepared ahead for this light, tangy dessert. The syrup can be made and reheated, and the rolls can be either chilled or frozen and fried to finish. To insure a light, crisp result, the oil should be hot, and the rolls drained on plenty of paper towels after frying.

SERVES 4–8

3 lemons, rinsed
3 limes, rinsed
1 tbsp finely chopped candied ginger
$^1\!/_2$ cup water
$^1\!/_3$ cup granulated sugar
1 tsp cornstarch
3 sheets filo pastry
$^3\!/_4$ cup finely diced pineapple
$^3\!/_4$ cup finely diced mango
1 tbsp cornstarch, mixed with enough cold
    water to make a paste
oil for deep frying (not olive oil)
shredded coconut, toasted lightly

1 First, make the syrup. Grate the rind and squeeze the juice from the lemons and limes, and put into a saucepan with the ginger, water and sugar. Bring to a boil, and simmer for 5 minutes.

2 Put the 1 teaspoon of cornstarch into a small bowl, and add a little water to make a paste. Stir in about $^1\!/_4$ cup of the syrup. Combine well, and return to the saucepan. Bring to a boil, stirring. Remove from the heat, and cover.

3 Spread out 1 sheet of the filo pastry on a counter, keeping the other 2 covered. Cut into 4-in. squares.

4 Put a teaspoonful of the fruit in the middle of each square, and roll up into a sausage shape, tucking the ends in. Seal the ends with the cornstarch paste.

5 Pour the oil to a depth of $2^1\!/_2$ in. into a deep skillet or wok and heat until it is 350°–375°F, or a cube of bread browns in 30 seconds. Have ready a plate or baking sheet lined with paper towels. Deep-fry the rolls until golden-brown, 2–3 minutes. Remove with a perforated spoon, and drain on the paper towels. Keep warm while you fry the remaining rolls.

6 Put the shredded coconut on a plate and roll each roll in it.

7 To serve, put 2 rolls on each plate, surrounded by the lemon and lime syrup.

STEP 2

STEP 3

STEP 4

STEP 6

STRAWBERRY MASCARPONE WITH SABLE COOKIES

A deliciously light dessert that would be a pleasure to eat at the end of a rich meal. The clean flavors would go very well after a beef roast.

SERVES 4

COOKIES:
1¼ cups all-purpose flour
5 tbsp superfine sugar
⅓ cup softened unsalted butter
1 tbsp water
1 egg yolk

STRAWBERRY MASCARPONE:
2 egg yolks
¼ cup superfine sugar
2 cups Mascarpone cheese
2 cups strawberries, hulled
2 egg whites
confectioners' sugar, to decorate

1 First, make the cookies. Sift the flour into a bowl, and stir in the sugar. Make a well in the center, and add the butter, water and egg yolk. Work with the fingertips until well blended, about 3 minutes. Roll into a ball, and wrap in baking parchment. Chill for 1 hour.

2 Roll out the dough on a floured counter until it is ¼ in. thick. Using a 2½-in. cutter, stamp out about 20 cookies.

3 Transfer the cookies to greased and floured or lined cookie sheets. Bake in a preheated oven at 350°F for 15–20 minutes. Transfer to a wire rack immediately.

4 Meanwhile, make the Strawberry Mascarpone. Beat together the egg yolks and sugar until pale.

5 Add the Mascarpone cheese, and beat well.

6 Blend the strawberries in a blender or food processor. Strain into a large bowl. Alternatively, mash the strawberries with a wooden spoon, and press through a strainer. Stir in the Mascarpone cheese mixture.

7 Beat the egg whites until stiff, and fold into the Mascarpone cheese mixture.

8 To serve, place 1 or 2 spoonfuls of the Mascarpone on each serving plate and put a few cookies by the side. Sprinkle with confectioners' sugar.

EXOTIC FRUIT SALAD

This is a sophisticated fruit salad that makes use of some of the exotic fruits that can now be seen in the supermarket. It is delicious served with pancakes.

STEP 3

SERVES 6

3 passion-fruit
1/2 cup superfine sugar
2/3 cup water
1 mango
10 lychees, canned or fresh
1 star-fruit

1 Halve the passion-fruit, and press the flesh through a strainer into a saucepan.

2 Add the sugar and water to the saucepan, and bring to a gentle boil, stirring frequently.

3 Put the mango on its side on a cutting board, and cut a thick slice from each side, cutting as near to the pit as possible. Cut away as much flesh as possible in large chunks from the pit section.

4 Take the 2 side slices, and make 3 cuts through the flesh but not the skin, and 3 more at right angles to make a lattice pattern.

5 Push the skin inside out, so that the cubed flesh is exposed and you can easily cut it off in large chunks.

6 Peel and pit the lychees, and cut the star-fruit into 12 slices.

7 Add all the mango flesh, the lychees and the star-fruit to the passion-fruit and sugar syrup, and poach slowly for 5 minutes. Remove the fruit with a perforated spoon.

8 Bring the sugar syrup to a boil, and cook for 5 minutes until it thickens slightly.

9 To serve, transfer all the fruit to a warmed serving bowl or individual serving glasses, pour over the sugar syrup, and serve warm, but not hot.

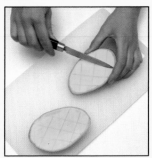

STEP 4

STEP 5

CARDAMOM CREAM

A delicious accompaniment to any exotic fruit dish is cardamom cream. Crush the seeds from 8 cardamom pods. Add 1 1/4 cups whipping cream, and whip until soft peaks form.

STEP 7

STEP 2

STEP 3

STEP 4

STEP 5

MANGO MOUSSE

This delicious and exotic mousse can also be made with other tropical fruit such as papaya, pineapple or bananas.

SERVES 6–8

4 large ripe mangoes
1 passion-fruit
$1/3$ cup superfine sugar
$2^1/2$ cups thick natural yogurt or $1^1/4$ cups
thick natural yogurt and $1^1/4$ cups
heavy cream

1 To prepare the mango, set it on its side on a cutting board and cut a thick slice from each side, cutting as near to the pit as possible. Cut as much flesh away from the pit as possible, in large chunks. Take the 2 side slices and make 3 cuts through the skin but not the flesh, and make 3 more at right angles to make a lattice pattern. Push the skin inside out, so that the cubed flesh is exposed, and you can easily cut it off in large chunks.

2 Cut the passion-fruit in half, and scoop out the flesh with a teaspoon. Strain this, and add it to the mango flesh.

3 Sprinkle the fruit with the sugar, and let rest for 15–20 minutes.

4 Mash the fruit or purée in a food processor or blender until smooth. Set aside a few spoonfuls for decoration.

5 Fold in the thick natural yogurt, and blend well. Whip the cream, if using, and fold it into the mixture.

6 Chill the mousse for at least 2 hours until set. Spoon over the reserved fruit purée to serve.

MANGOES

Finding a really good mango in fruit stores and supermarkets is quite an art. They are usually imported underripe and, as they don't have a chance to mature in the sun, may lose some of their sweetness and flavor. Even if they look and feel right, the flesh may be disappointingly stringy or chalky. Look out for Bombay mangoes which are the best I've ever eaten; they are available all year round, although they are at their peak in March and April. Canned mangoes in syrup are a very good alternative if fresh ones are hard to find.

STEP 1

STEP 3

STEP 5

STEP 6

GRAPE & RICOTTA CHEESECAKE

A light and delicious cheesecake that is straightforward to make, and quick to disappear.

SERVES 6

³/₄ cup crushed graham crackers
1 cup crushed ratafia or amaretti cookies
¹/₃ cup melted and cooled unsalted butter
1 tbsp or envelope powdered gelatin
¹/₂ cup heavy cream
1¹/₄ cups Ricotta cheese
2 tbsp mixed candied peel
2 tbsp clear honey
¹/₄ tsp vanilla extract
3 cups green seedless grapes, washed

1 Combine the crackers, cookies and butter. Press into the bottom of 6 ramekins or glasses, or into an 8-in. springform pan, and chill.

2 Put 3 tablespoons of hot water into a heatproof bowl. Sprinkle on the powdered gelatin and stir. Set over a pan of barely simmering water, and let dissolve. When it becomes clear, it is ready to use.

3 Whip the cream until stiff. Combine the Ricotta cheese, mixed candied peel, honey and vanilla extract in a separate bowl. Stir this mixture into the heavy cream. Do not over-stir.

4 Stir the dissolved gelatin into the Ricotta mixture.

5 Halve the grapes. Divide half of them between the ramekins, glasses or pan, arranging neatly on top of the cracker and cookie layer.

6 Spoon the Ricotta mixture over the top. Arrange the remaining grapes attractively on the top. Chill for 2 hours, or until set.

7 To serve, remove the outer ring from the springform pan, or put the ramekins on small plates.

VARIATION

The grapes in this recipe can be replaced by black grapes or any other fruit. Remember, however, that bananas will go brown. Either canned or fresh apricots are particularly nice with this cheesecake.

CHAPTER FIVE

Special Occasion Desserts

What party would be complete without a grand finale, a dish that shows off your skills and sends your guests away satisfied and eager to return? Party desserts deserve a lot of effort and often need some advance preparation, but it will be worth it when you present your creation to your admiring guests.

When you are making your shopping list, think about how you will present the dish – which fruit to decorate it with, whether to use some confectionery or cake decorations, and perhaps a ribbon – anything to give it a bit of glamor! And think about the serving plate – I'm all for showing off the best china and bringing the best dishes out of the cupboard for such a special dessert – it is a compliment to your guests when you go to such trouble to entertain them!

STEP 1

STEP 3

STEP 4

STEP 7

CREME BRULEE

This is the classic recipe that everybody loves! The title simply means "burned cream."

SERVES 4

4 egg yolks
2½ cups heavy cream
⅓ cup light brown sugar

1 Beat the egg yolks until pale.

2 Put the cream into a saucepan, and set over a medium heat. Bring it to boiling point for about 30 seconds.

3 Pour the cream onto the egg yolks, whisking all the time.

4 Return the cream and yolks to the saucepan. Set over a low heat, and stir until thickened, about 5 minutes.

5 Pour into 4 individual ramekins or 1 large serving dish. Chill for 4 hours or overnight.

6 Sprinkle the brûlée with the light brown sugar to a thickness of about ¼ in.

7 Place under a preheated very hot broiler, until the sugar has caramelized to a golden-brown. This takes about 3 minutes, depending on the heat of the broiler, how far away from the broiler the brûlée is, and how thick the sugar is. Let cool before serving.

HANDY HINT

You may have seen a lozenge-shaped piece of iron on the end of a long handle in cookware stores. This is a brûlée iron. It is usually about 3 in. round, and is designed to be held flat over the brûlée, after being heated to a very high temperature over a flame or electric hot plate. The thickness of the iron means that it stays hot for a few minutes, long enough to caramelize the sugar.

STEP 1

STEP 2

STEP 3

STEP 4

HOT MOCHA SOUFFLE

Soufflés are not difficult as long as your recipe is failsafe, and the mixture is right before you put it in the oven. The sauce here is a delightful addition to the recipe.

SERVES 6

butter for greasing
2 tbsp superfine sugar
2 egg yolks
3 tsp confectioners' sugar
2 tsp all-purpose flour
5 squares dark chocolate, melted
2 tsp instant coffee powder, dissolved in
  1 tbsp hot water
4 egg whites
confectioners' sugar, to decorate

SAUCE:
¼ cup granulated sugar
¼ cup water
3½ squares dark chocolate
1 tbsp instant coffee powder
⅓ cup whipping cream

1 Butter a 3½-cup soufflé dish. Dust with the superfine sugar, and tap out any excess.

2 Beat the egg yolks until pale, and sift in the confectioners' sugar.

3 Stir in the flour, melted chocolate and dissolved coffee.

4 Wrap a piece of baking parchment around the soufflé dish, to an inch above the rim of the dish. Secure with string or an elastic band.

5 Beat the egg whites until just stiff, and fold into the soufflé mixture.

6 Pour the mixture into the soufflé dish right up to the rim. Run the tip of a knife quickly between the soufflé and the edge of the dish. Bake in a preheated oven at 350°F for 45 minutes. Do not open the oven.

7 Make the sauce. Put the sugar and water into a saucepan. Simmer until dissolved, then add the chocolate, instant coffee powder and cream. Keep warm until ready to serve.

8 To serve, transfer the sauce to a warmed serving jug and, working quickly, remove the parchment from the soufflé dish; sift over the confectioners' sugar, and take to the table before it sinks. Make a hole in the top of the soufflé by stabbing it with a knife, and pour in the sauce, preferably from a great height!

STEP 2

STEP 4

STEP 5

STEP 6

CHOCOLATE MARQUIS

A fabulously rich dessert that needs only a smidgen on each plate. If you feel it needs something else, serve with crème fraîche or fresh fruit and make chocolate leaves to decorate.

SERVES 6–8

1 pound dark chocolate
¼ cup unsalted butter
2 tbsp superfine sugar
4 whole eggs
1 tbsp all-purpose flour
cocoa powder (optional)

1 Line an 8-in. springform pan with baking parchment.

2 Melt the chocolate, butter and half of the sugar together in a heatproof bowl, set over a saucepan of barely simmering water.

3 Beat the eggs and remaining sugar together until pale.

4 Fold in the flour carefully. Pour the chocolate mixture on top of the eggs and stir in gently with a wooden spoon.

5 Fold together with a whisk, lightly, but until well combined.

6 Pour the mixture into the lined pan and bake in a preheated oven at 450°F for 12 minutes only. It should still be slightly wobbly in the center.

7 Run a knife around the edge, release the pan, and replace. Let cool. Freeze for at least 2 hours or until required.

8 To serve, remove at least an hour before serving to let the dessert come to room temperature. Dust with cocoa powder, if using.

CHOCOLATE LEAVES

Chocolate leaves make a very attractive decoration on the plate. Select some prettily shaped leaves from the garden, and rinse them well. Drain and pat them dry with paper towels – they must be completely dry. Melt some chocolate in a double boiler or in a heatproof bowl set over a saucepan of gently simmering water. Use a grease-free paintbrush to brush the underside of the leaves with the melted chocolate. Make sure that the chocolate is thick where the leaf meets the stalk. Paint on 2 or 3 layers, just waiting briefly for the chocolate to dry between each layer. Spread them out on a tray to dry, and put them into the freezer for 10 minutes to harden. When you are ready to use the leaves, simply peel the leaf from the chocolate.

STEP 3

STEP 4

STEP 5

STEP 6

BAKED ALASKA

This is another old favorite, and is a very impressive presentation that can be whipped up (literally!) at the last moment, and presented to admiring gasps.

SERVES 4–6

¹/₂ cup softened butter
¹/₂ cup superfine sugar
2 eggs, lightly beaten
1 cup self-rising flour
2 tbsp brandy or sherry
2 tbsp raspberry jam
3¹/₂ cups vanilla or raspberry ripple ice
    cream – do not use "soft scoop" ice cream

MERINGUE:
4 egg whites
¹/₃ cup superfine sugar

1 Grease and flour an 8-in. layer pan.

2 Beat the butter and sugar together, until pale and fluffy. Beat in the eggs gradually. If the mixture starts to separate while you are doing this, add a little flour before continuing.

3 Fold in the flour carefully but thoroughly, and pour the mixture into the greased pan. Bake in a preheated oven at 375°F for 40 minutes. Transfer to a wire rack to cool.

4 About 30 minutes before serving, transfer the sponge to an ovenproof serving dish, trimming to fit if necessary. Sprinkle with the brandy or sherry, and spread with the jam. Freeze for 20 minutes.

5 If the ice cream block is not round, transfer it to a plate, and re-form it to the shape of your dish, using foil or baking parchment,

6 Remove the sponge from the freezer, and put the ice cream on top. Refreeze until 10 minutes before ready to serve.

7 To make the meringue, beat the egg whites until stiff. Add the sugar gradually, and continue beating until stiff and glossy.

8 Take the sponge and ice cream from the freezer, and spoon the meringue over the top to cover the ice cream completely. Use the back of the spoon to form peaks all over it. Work quickly so the ice cream does not melt.

9 Bake in a preheated oven at 450°F for 5 minutes only. Keep an eye on it, as the meringue burns easily. Remove and serve immediately before the ice cream has a chance to melt!

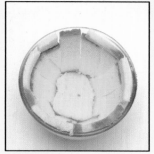

STEP 2

STEP 3

STEP 4

STEP 4

ZUCCOTTO

A delicious Italian trifle, very rich and very delicious! It can be prepared ahead and stored in the freezer, but remove at least 1 hour before serving so that it is relatively soft to eat.

SERVES 6–8

14-ounce can pitted black cherries, drained, or 1 pound fresh black cherries, pitted
2 tbsp maraschino
2 tbsp water
6½ in. pound cake, thinly sliced, or 20 ladyfingers
3 tbsp orange-flavored liqueur
2½ cups heavy cream
⅓ cup superfine sugar
¼ tsp vanilla extract
scant ⅓ cup mixed candied peel
2 tbsp ground almonds
3 squares dark chocolate, melted
2 tbsp rum
½ cup chopped hazelnuts

1 Put the cherries into a saucepan with the maraschino and water. Bring to a boil. Remove from the heat, and let steep for 10 minutes.

2 Line the sides of a round 3-cup bowl with the sliced cake or ladyfingers. Drain the cherries, and use the juice to moisten the sponge. Sprinkle the liqueur over the sponge. Put into the freezer.

3 Whip one third of the cream until stiff, and stir in half of the sugar, the vanilla extract, candied peel and ground almonds. Spread this mixture in a layer over the sponge bottom and up the sides. Return to the freezer for about 40 minutes until firm.

4 Whip one third of the cream until softly stiff, and fold in the cooled melted chocolate, the rum and hazelnuts. Spread this in a layer over the cream layer, and return to the freezer.

5 Blend the cherries in a food processor, or mash well by hand, and stir in the remaining sugar. Whip the remaining cream until stiff, and fold in the cherries. Fill the center of the bowl with this. Return to the freezer for 1 hour, or until ready to serve. If it is kept for longer than 2 hours in the freezer, remove 1 hour before serving. If you do not have a freezer, add a little powdered gelatin to the zuccotto. Dissolve 2 tablespoons or envelopes of powdered gelatin in ½ cup of hot water in a bowl set over a saucepan of simmering water. Stir a third of this into each layer.

6 To serve, unmold onto a chilled dish and decorate as you wish.

STEP 2

STEP 3

STEP 5

STEP 6

PAVLOVA

This fruit meringue dish was created for Anna Pavlova, and it looks very impressive. Be sure to use some of the fabulous fruits that are now available all year round, to make a colorful fruit display.

SERVES 8

6 egg whites
1/2 tsp cream of tartar
1 cup superfine sugar
1 tsp vanilla extract
1 1/4 cups whipping cream
2 1/2 cups hulled and halved strawberries
3 tbsp orange-flavored liqueur
fruit of your choice to decorate

1 Line a cookie sheet with baking parchment, and mark out a round to fit your serving plate. The recipe makes enough meringue for a 12-in. round.

2 Beat the egg whites and cream of tartar together until stiff. Gradually beat in the superfine sugar and vanilla extract. Beat well until glossy and stiff.

3 Either spoon or pipe the meringue mixture into the marked round, in an even layer, slightly raised at the edges, to form a dip in the center.

4 Baking the meringue depends on your preference. If you like a soft chewy meringue, bake at 275°F for about 1 1/2 hours until dry but slightly soft in the center. If you prefer a dry

meringue, bake in the oven at 225°F for 3 hours until dry.

5 When you are ready to serve, whip the cream to a piping consistency, and either spoon or pipe onto the meringue base, leaving a border of meringue all around the edge.

6 Stir the strawberries and liqueur together, and spoon onto the cream. Cover the meringue with fruit of your choice, such as whole strawberries or slices of star-fruit, pineapple, and apple. Serve immediately.

MAKING A DRY MERINGUE

I prefer a dry meringue, and I leave it in the oven, on the lowest setting, overnight – however, I wouldn't recommend using this technique with a gas oven. In an electric oven or solid fuel stove it would be fine.

PERFECT PUDDINGS

There are a number of basic ingredients that are regularly used in the making of puddings and desserts. Here is some detailed information about a few of them, which will help your puddings to turn out perfectly.

EGGS
Freshness
Eggs can be used up to 3–4 weeks after laying. However, it is difficult to tell from the date on the box how fresh an egg is, as they may have been laid some time before packing.

A simple way to identify a really fresh egg is to hold it close to your ear – there will be no discernible movement. If it is a little older, you will hear some movement. However, this is not an exact indication of its age, only a rough guide, and the egg is fit to eat even if you can hear some movement.

A new-laid egg fills the entire shell, and as it ages, the air pocket at the broader end expands. This is the basis for the flotation test. A new-laid egg will lie on the bottom of a bowl of water; the older it is, the higher one end will sit in the water, until at 2–3 weeks old it is standing upright on the base of the bowl. If the whole egg floats, it should be discarded.

Storage
Egg shells are porous, so eggs should not be stored near strong-smelling food.

THE HISTORY OF PUDDINGS
At the conclusion of a meal when our appetites are usually satisfied and our palates content, a dessert offers a chance to indulge in something eaten purely for pleasure rather than nutrition, and offers the cook a chance to be creative and show off a little imagination and expertise.

The dessert course can take many forms. Sometimes a simple fruit bowl, filled with a variety of familiar and exotic fruits, is often enough; alternatively, fruit can be macerated in sugar to bring out the full flavors and then served adorned with cream. At the other extreme a skillful assembly of beautifully baked sponge cake, frozen cream and quickly cooked snowy egg white is designed to impress and will satisfy the eye and the mouth, as well as the cook's creative tendencies.

Desserts were not always so wide-ranging. Cakes, pies, and cookies, usually sweetened with molasses or maple syrup, were among the early favorites, but it was not until refined sugar became more easily available that cooks and chefs began to devise ways to demonstrate their skills in creative cooking. This often resulted in elaborate presentations of fruit gelatins and table creams, layered in different colors and molded into fanciful shapes, designed to impress the eye more than satisfy the palate.

Gradually sugar became an everyday ingredient rather than a luxury item, and we became more used to consuming it as part of our daily diet. Different sorts of candy soon became common, and a wide variety of puddings began to appear regularly on restaurant menus and on the family dinner table.

THE MODERN DESSERT
Depending on your preference, or the occasion, the dessert can be a light finish to a heavy meal, or a grand finale to a complex and creative meal. You may need to cater for children's simpler tastes at a family meal, whereas at an adult dinner table, something more sophisticated is called for. I know some cooks who never present less than three desserts, and I have to say that I also enjoy the preparation and decoration that goes into the dessert course – it is an opportunity to show off your skill in the kitchen, and delight your guests. It can also be very satisfying to spend time creating a delicious and impressive looking soufflé or gâteau.

The season is a factor too, of course. There is nothing nicer in the middle of winter than to finish a simple meal with a hot dessert, where the dessert is actually providing some of the meal's nutritional content. The Italian Bread & Butter Pudding and the Raisin & Nut Pudding in the Hot Puddings chapter are both ideal for this, as is the Cherry Clafoutis in the Quick & Easy chapter.

Although most berries are available all year round, fresh or frozen, they taste best when eaten at the height of summer with only a sprinkling of sugar.

A Baked Alaska will delight at any time of the year – children are especially thrilled to cut into the crisp meringue and find ice cream in the middle!

There is something here for the chocaholics among you – for a quick fix, try the Chocolate Coconut Layer, or for something worth some extra effort, the Chocolate Marquis is fabulous!

When presenting rich desserts, I find that a large plate of fruit, peeled and cut, goes down extremely well as a refresher and palate cleanser. Many restaurants serve a light fruit sorbet for the same reason.

INGREDIENTS

Even though we eat a huge variety of sweet and sugar products nowadays, the main ingredients for a dessert are usually varying amounts of a few basic items, which are discussed below, with alternatives suggested where appropriate. Sometimes we need to satisfy a sweet tooth or create a dessert without stocking up on calories and cholesterol, and there are usually substitutes that can be used instead of the richer ingredients. I have detailed these below.

Butter

When baking or cooking with fat, butter has the finest flavor. It is best to use unsalted butter as an ingredient in puddings and desserts, unless stated otherwise in the recipe. Margarine can be substituted for butter if you prefer. However, do not use a "low-fat spread" as a substitute, as most of them are not suitable for cooking with, especially if you are baking the dish; the ingredients will often simply separate. Use plain margarine or a similar product, which states on the package that it is suitable for baking. In some instances margarine will be more suitable, as it creams with sugar more pleasantly than butter.

Chocolate

There are chefs called *chocolatiers* who devote their working lives to perfecting the art of cooking with chocolate, creating desserts, sauces, confectionery, decorations, and even chocolate sculptures. However, you do not need a lifetime's experience to use chocolate to great effect.

Avoid using cake-covering products, as they will ruin the taste of your desserts. When testing these recipes, I used a good-quality dark or white eating chocolate. Supermarkets' own brands are usually of a good quality too. The chocolate that professional *chocolatiers* use is called *couverture* chocolate, and is sold in large blocks. There are small bars of *couverture* available in some supermarkets, labeled *Chocolat Meunier*. The advantage of using this chocolate is that it has a higher cocoa solids content, and is therefore more stable to work with, and has a more satisfying chocolate taste.

Good-quality white chocolate has no cocoa solids content, only cocoa butter, which makes it a little more tricky to work with, but if you follow the recipe you won't have a problem.

To melt chocolate, first break it into pieces. I do this by leaving the chocolate in the package and banging it on the

Usage

Fresher eggs are more suitable for poaching and frying, as they stay more compact and the white is thicker in consistency. Older eggs are no less nutritious, but are better kept for baking and sauces, where appearance is not necessarily a consideration, as the white of the egg becomes more fluid and watery.

Duck and goose eggs are eminently suitable for baking as they have a higher fat content than hen eggs. They are about one-third larger, which should be taken into account when using them in place of hen eggs.

Beating

There is no trick or mystery to beating egg whites to a maximum foam, but the best results are obtained if a few simple precautions are taken.

First, separate the egg whites from the yolks by dropping the whites into a small bowl, then transferring each white to the whisking bowl as you go. This insures that any stray bits of egg yolk will spoil only one white.

The foam is formed by air being enveloped by the protein in the egg white. Acid helps the protein to stretch and make a larger volume of foam, which is why a pinch of cream of tartar is often added at the beginning of beating.

A hand-held balloon whisk gets the best results from egg

whites, whereas electric mixers do the job quickly and efficiently, but without creating as much volume as a balloon whisk would.

You should select a large bowl, so that there is enough space for you to beat, and for the whites to expand, and make sure the bowl is free of grease. Many chefs use unlined copper bowls to beat in, as a harmless chemical reaction between the copper and egg whites creates a stronger and more stable foam.

Start by beating slowly in a figure-of-eight pattern until the whites are a mass of bubbles, then speed up your beating, lifting and enveloping air as you go. When the whisk leaves a soft peak when it is lifted, the whites are the right consistency for folding into most mixtures, including soufflés and omelets. If you are using the whites for meringues, carry on beating until the whisk leaves a stiff peak behind. Do not stop beating once you have started, and be careful not to overbeat the whites – they will become grainy and unusable.

If you are adding sugar, beat it in gradually until the whites are stiff and glossy. Use the beaten whites immediately so that they lose no air.

counter a few times. Obviously the smaller the pieces, the quicker they will melt.

Use a plastic, pyrex, or ceramic bowl to melt the chocolate in – a metal bowl can be used, but it often gets too hot, and for this reason needs constant attention. The bowl must be set over a saucepan so that it fits tightly at the top; this prevents steam from escaping and dripping into the chocolate, which will make the chocolate "seize" or become granular, at which point it must be abandoned, as it cannot be restored.

Chocolate can also be melted in the microwave on High Power, and should be stirred every 30 seconds.

When adding other ingredients to melted chocolate, avoid adding alcohol first to neat chocolate; add the other ingredients first, and the alcohol last. If for some reason you have to add alcohol first, pour it all in at once, and stir constantly until smooth.

Cocoa powder

This can be used as a flavoring in place of chocolate, but the liquid content of the dish must be increased to compensate. This is usually done by adding milk, as milk has a fat content that helps to create the right consistency.

Cream

This most delicious ingredient comes in various forms:

Clotted cream – This was once available only in the West Country of England, but is now exported to some gourmet stores in the US. It has a 55 percent fat content,

and is very thick. It is suitable for serving with a wide variety of desserts, and in Cornwall is sometimes served with ice cream!

Crème fraîche – This is a cream product that is becoming more popular. Originally from France, it has a slightly sour nutty taste, and is very thick. It is suitable for cooking, but has the same fat content as heavy cream. It can be made by stirring cultured buttermilk into heavy cream and refrigerating the mixture overnight.

Half-and-half – This is suitable only for adding to coffee and for pouring over desserts, but not for cooking. It has a $10^{1}/_{2}$–18 percent fat content.

Heavy cream – This is the only cream that can be safely boiled without curdling. Typically it is 36–40 percent saturated fat, which is bad news for people who have to monitor cholesterol levels – there are substitutes suggested below. Heavy cream can be whipped to a large volume, but "extra thick" heavy cream is not suitable for whipping.

Light cream – This is the type of cream most commonly used for cooking; however, this kind of cream should not be boiled, as it will curdle. Also, always add hot liquids to the cream rather than the cream to the liquids, to avoid curdling. Light cream can be stirred into cake mixes, and poured onto desserts and into coffee. Unpasteurized cream has a lot more flavor than the modern pasteurized version, but is only available direct from